MOONBOWS & Alligator RAIN

ISABEL THOMAS

Collins

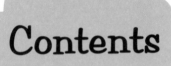

Contents

Chapter 1
A recipe for weather

Yesterday was freezing cold.
My teammates all complained.
But other teams were splashing round
in alligator rain!

Today the weather's windy.
It's hard to catch and throw.
But other teams were stuck inside
watching thundersnow!

Tomorrow should be sunny.
The game's been rearranged.
Unless the weather steals the show
by doing something strange!

Look outside. Look up at the sky.
What's the **weather** like today?

Perhaps you can see blue sky or clouds.

Perhaps you can see lightning, hailstones or
a tornado.

Perhaps you can see moonbows, thundersnow or
alligator rain!

Weather is what you see when you look out of the window and up at the sky. There are hundreds of different kinds of weather.
Some are common. Some are rare. Some only happen in certain parts of the world. But they all begin with the same three things:

air + water + the sun's energy = weather

How can these three things cause so many different types of weather?

Let's take a closer look.

Air on the move

Air is almost everywhere. When it's still, we forget it's there. But air never stays still for long.

When the Sun is shining, everything on Earth's surface warms up. The air next to the surface gets warmer too. What happens to warm air? It rises!

Try this!

You can't see moving air, but you can see the effect it has on other things.

Tear tissue paper into thin strips.

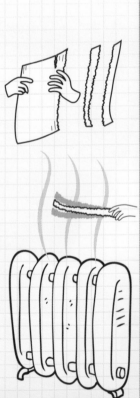

Hold them above a warm radiator. You might see the tissue paper flutter!

This happens because warm air spreads out and takes up more space. This makes the warm air lighter than the cooler air around it. The warm air rises up, and pushes on the thin tissue paper.

Air that has been warmed by the Sun also rises. Cooler air from somewhere else rushes in to fill the space left behind. We call this moving air "wind".

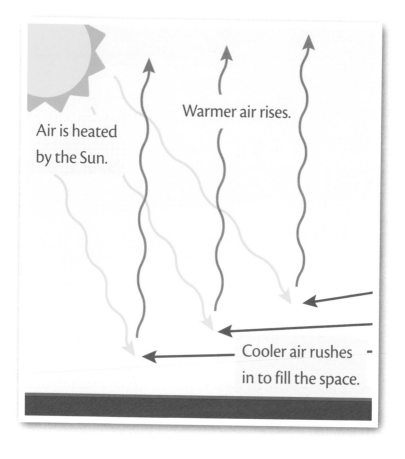

Air is heated by the Sun.

Warmer air rises.

Cooler air rushes in to fill the space.

Wind can lift kites or topple trees. It can make us shiver on a cold day or cool us down on a hot day. We can use the wind to turn windmills and push sailing boats. Animals also use the wind to travel.

Some spiderlings (baby spiders) and caterpillars climb to the tip of a twig and spin a thread of silk. This catches the wind like a tiny parachute and carries the spiderling to a new home.

silver-Y moth

Many butterflies and moths hitch a ride on fast-moving winds. They can travel as fast as a car on a motorway!

Albatrosses use the wind to fly for days without flapping their wings. This saves energy.

waved albatross

9

Water on the move

When air is warmed by the Sun, it rises.
When water is warmed by the Sun, it can change form altogether!

The Sun's heat warms water on the land, in lakes and seas, and in the leaves of plants. Some of the water changes into a gas called water vapour.

Try this!

Water vapour is invisible, but you can prove that it's there in the air. Breathe onto a mirror or a window. The water vapour in your warm breath cools when it touches the glass. It turns back into tiny droplets of liquid water, which cling to the glass and make it look misty.

As warm air rises, it carries invisible water vapour up high into the sky. Up there it is much cooler. The water vapour begins to cool and changes back into liquid water. It forms tiny droplets that clump together as clouds.

The most common clouds are stratocumulus clouds, which means "flattened heaps". They have a flat bottom and fluffy, rounded tops and can be white or grey. They hang around in the sky together in clumps, with small gaps in between.

Isn't it weird that ...

clouds have flat bottoms!

Water vapour only turns into clouds when the air is cool enough. This happens at a certain height above the ground. The bottom of clouds marks this invisible line, where the air can't hold water anymore. Below the line, there is no cloud because the water vapour is still warm enough to be gas. The tops of clouds are usually fluffy, not flat, because new cloud keeps pushing the older cloud upwards.

Just like air, clouds are always on the move. Watch the wind moving clouds across the sky. Some clouds drift by up high. Others roll along closer to the ground.

The wind can carry clouds far from the place they formed. Clouds that formed over sea might be blown over land. Fog that formed over mountains might be blown across deserts.

But clouds don't stay in the sky forever ...

Cloud spotting

Use this picture to name
the clouds that you spot.

cirrostratus
misty, milky
high clouds

altocumulus
rolling clouds

nimbostratus
large, deep, dark
clouds

cumulus
flat-bottomed,
fluffy-topped
clouds

stratus
forms a thick
blanket of
cloud

cirrocumulus
rippling high clouds

cirrus
wispy high clouds
that curve like
horses' tails

altostratus
pale grey clouds that
block sunlight from
casting shadows

cumulonimbus
towering piles of
dark thunderclouds

stratocumulus
fluffy white clouds like
cotton wool in the sky

Rare clouds

Some types of clouds
are very rare.
How many can
you collect?

Name lenticular
Look like flying saucers,
pancakes
Form when wind blows
across mountains
Features reveals the shape of
"ripples" in the air

Name arcus
Look like they are rolling along
Form when a powerful
thunderstorm is on the way
Features long, thin and dark

Name noctilucent
Look like night-shining clouds
Form so high in the sky that
light still reaches them after
the sun sets
Features glow blue or silver in
the dark

Name mammatus
Look like a cloud turned upside down
Form just before hail or snow falls from a cloud
Features bulge at the bottom

Name nacreous
Look like mother-of-pearl on the inside of a shell
Form from ice crystals in very cold places near the Poles
Features shimmer when the Sun is low in the sky

Name virga
Look like jellyfish
Form when rain or snow warms up and changes back into water vapour before it hits the ground
Features fluffy tops and glowing "tentacles"

Name banner
Look like a flag on a pole
Form on the less windy side of hills and mountains
Features cling to the mountainside, staying in one place

17

Chapter 2
Water falls from the sky

Rain

is the end of a story

that begins with water in a distant sea:

warmed by sunshine, lifted by air

collected in clouds, carried on the wind,
until it falls

drop   plop

     by   plop

       drop   plop

into a playground puddle, where
the story starts again.

Which of these things have you seen falling from the sky?

snow

sleet

rain

alligators

hail

Clouds are always changing. Their tiny droplets of water grow bigger and bigger. Eventually, the water droplets become so heavy they fall from the sky. Scientists use the word **precipitation** for any kind of water falling from the sky. Precipitation can be liquid water (rain), frozen water (snow or hail) or a mixture of both (sleet).

Grab your umbrella. Let's take a closer look at precipitation.

Strange rain

Inside a cloud, most raindrops begin to grow around tiny specks of dust. This means rain isn't pure water. There is always dust, soot, or **pollen** mixed in. Sometimes, it changes the colour of the rain.

Yellow rain

Have you ever seen a thin layer of yellow or brown dust on windows or cars, after rain has dried? It could be sand from the Sahara Desert in Africa! Most dust that falls with rain in the UK has travelled thousands of kilometres from the Sahara.

Red rain

Bright red rain, known as blood rain, is very rare. It happens when lots of red dust or tiny germs get mixed with rain clouds.

Black rain

When a volcano erupts or a huge fire breaks out, black soot ends up mixed with water in clouds. This can cause black rain! Pollution from factories can stain the rain, too. In the 1800s, factories in England and Scotland released so much soot that sheep were painted black by the rain!

Strange snow

Snowflakes are tiny crystals of ice, falling from frozen clouds. Most ice crystals melt as they fall to the ground, turning into rain or sleet on their way down. On a very cold day, when the air near the ground is below two degrees Celsius, snowflakes make it all the way to the ground. As they fall, more water freezes onto the snowflake. The snowflake grows. Snowflakes are always symmetrical, with six sides or arms.

Isn't it weird that ...
Snowflakes are beautiful!

As droplets of water freeze, they can form beautiful, regular patterns. If you look at a snowflake under a microscope, you can see these patterns. Each snowflake grows as it falls, and each journey is different – so each snowflake has a different pattern.

Waves, spikes and balls

Snow can form strange patterns on
the ground, too. In flat, windy places such as
Antarctica, waves of snow form to look just like
sand dunes. In high, dry places such as the Andes
mountains, snow forms sharp-looking spikes as
it thaws. When snow falls on a shore, the waves
can roll it into thousands of natural snowballs!

Strangest of all are snow doughnuts. These rare
shapes form when a clump of snow falls off a tree
branch and begins to roll down
a slope. They look like
huge, rolling
doughnuts!

Strange hail

Hailstones form during thunderstorms when strong winds suddenly lift raindrops high into the sky. It's so cold up high that the raindrops freeze solid. They grow bigger as more water freezes around them. Soon they are so heavy, they fall to the ground. Hailstones fall so quickly they don't have time to melt on the way down.

Hailstones can be as small as peas or as large as grapefruit! Large hailstones are very dangerous. In 2019, huge hailstones damaged thousands of homes and cars in Europe.

Hailstones are never perfect spheres. They are often lumpy or shaped like a rugby ball. Some even have horns or spikes!

What happens next?

Rain puddles don't stay on the ground forever. They vanish after a few hours or days. Snow and hail also melt and disappear. What happens to this water?

Some of it soaks into the ground. Some runs into streams and rivers, collecting in ponds, lakes and seas. The rest slowly turns back into water vapour. It ends up back in clouds high above the ground.

The journey of water from Earth's surface to clouds and back again never ends. Because the water travels round and round, it's called the water cycle.

Earth never gets any new water. The same water journeys through the water cycle again and again. This means that the water you drink today may once have been sipped by a Viking queen, a Roman gladiator, or a diplodocus!

clouds release water droplets

rain water flows into rivers and then into lakes or the sea

Precipitation tops up lakes, reservoirs, and underground sources of water. The water cycle means that plants and animals always have a supply of fresh water.

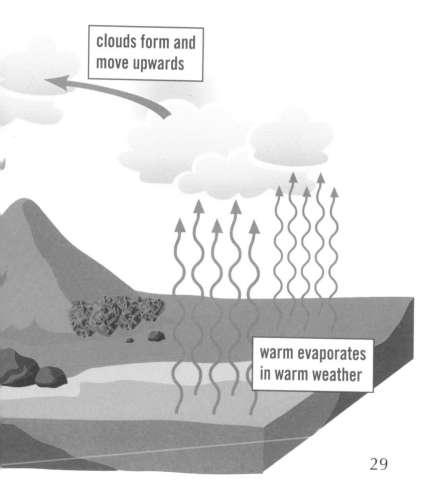

clouds form and
move upwards

warm evaporates
in warm weather

Alligator rain

Sometimes, precipitation brings
unexpected visitors. Occasionally, animals
get sucked up into the air by
powerful winds.

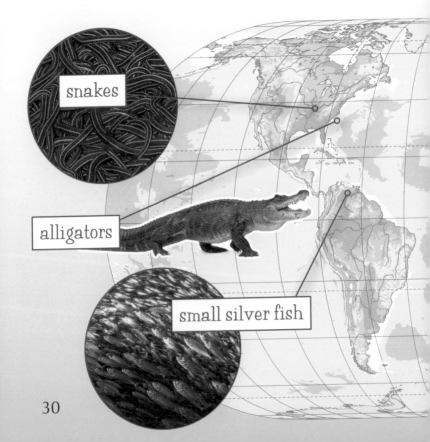

snakes

alligators

small silver fish

They can be blown many kilometres from their homes before raining back down to Earth!

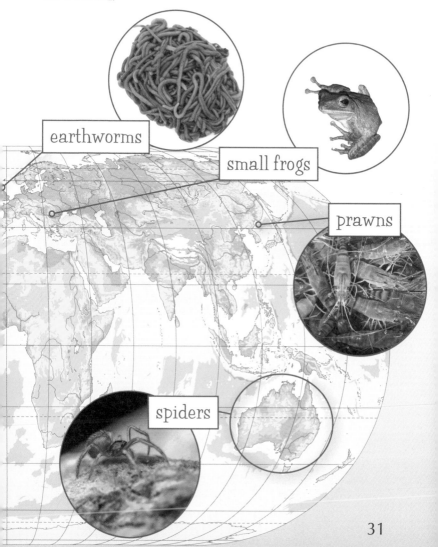

earthworms

small frogs

prawns

spiders

Chapter 3
Thunderstorms

Wind is almost everywhere
Rustling leaves and ruffling hair.

Chasing clouds across the sky
Alarming birds that squawk and cry.

Bringing rain that pours and pours
Whipping up waves that crash
on shores.

Stirring storms that blast and blow
Driving blizzards of frozen snow.

Causing lightning strikes – beware!
Wind is almost everywhere.

Weather is caused by air and water on the move. When winds are moving very quickly, they can bring stormy weather. Strong winds are one sign of a storm. Storms often bring heavy rain, hail, and thunder and lightning, too.

How do thunderstorms start?

On a sunny day, lots of warm air and water vapour can rise very quickly, forming towering cumulonimbus clouds. These can grow many kilometres tall. As air and ice crystals move up and down inside these huge clouds, they rub together and form static electricity.

Try this!

You can make static electricity yourself.

Rub a balloon against your hair. Then move the balloon slowly away from your head. You may see your hair moving towards the balloon. When two things that don't conduct electricity rub together, like the balloon and your hair, static electricity builds up. This is what makes your hair and the balloon attracted to each other.

So much static electricity builds up in thunderclouds, they become a bit like giant batteries in the sky. If static electricity gets the chance, it will flow to the ground. This is what happens during a thunderstorm. Every so often, there is a huge flash of lightning as electricity flows to the ground or to a different part of the cloud.

A large lightning flash inside a cloud or between two clouds is called sheet lightning. Forked lightning flashes between a cloud and the ground. Every second of every day, lightning strikes Earth's surface around 100 times!

It takes less than a second for a lightning bolt to heat up the air around it. For a moment, it becomes hotter than the surface of the Sun! The air explodes, causing a bright flash and the sound of thunder.

sheet lightning

forked lightning

Isn't it weird that ...

thunder comes after lightning!

Thunder is the sound that lightning makes. They are made at the same time, but light travels through air much faster than sound. Unless the storm is very close, the light reaches your eyes before the sound reaches your ears. Lightning bolts are just a couple of centimetres thick, but their path from cloud to ground can be many kilometres long. The sound caused by the nearest part of a lightning bolt will reach you first, followed by the sound caused by other parts, which is why thunder seems to rumble.

Try this!

Light and sound travel at fixed speeds through air, so you can use some simple maths to **estimate** how far away a storm is. Next time you see and hear a thunderstorm, count the number of seconds between a lightning flash and the sound of thunder it makes. Divide this number by three, and it will tell you how close the storm is in kilometres.

Strange storms

Sometimes, storms bring even stranger weather, including rare types of thunder and lightning!

Jellyfish sprites

As well as lightning, the static electricity that builds up in storm clouds can cause other strange weather. Jellyfish sprites are bright red or purple "tentacles" of light that form above storm clouds! They look like red or purple jellyfish in the night sky.

Ball lightning

You might spot strange lightning underneath thunderclouds too. Ball lightning looks like a colourful, glowing football rolling slowly through the air just above the ground. Unlike a football, it might make a hissing sound and a strange smell. The balls can roll through closed windows or the walls of houses and planes!

Thundersnow

Thunderstorms are more common in warm weather. When thunderstorms form in winter they can cause sudden heavy snow, known as thundersnow. Lightning looks brighter in this type of storm because the snowflakes act like millions of tiny mirrors, reflecting the light. However, the snow muffles the sound of the thunder. This is because snowflakes have lots of tiny pockets of air trapped in the ice, which soak up sound like a blanket. If the thunderstorm is more than a few kilometres away, you may not hear any thunder at all.

41

Tornadoes

Tornadoes are the fastest, fiercest storm winds on Earth. They begin when rising air starts to spin near the top of a towering thundercloud. The spinning column moves downwards, getting narrower and spinning faster. A funnel of spinning air forms below the cloud, with winds moving up to 480 kilometres per hour. This is faster than a bullet train!

If the bottom of the funnel touches the ground, it becomes a tornado. It starts to suck in dust, water and anything else in its path.

Tornadoes can be powerful enough to pick up lorries and even railway carriages, flinging them sideways.

Stuck in the doldrums

Hundreds of years ago, sailors relied on the wind – without any wind, sailing ships couldn't move. There was an area of the Pacific Ocean that was called the "doldrums" – there was very little wind there. This is part of a poem which describes what it was like to be "stuck in the doldrums".

Down dropped the breeze, the sails dropped down,
'Twas sad as sad could be;
And we did speak only to break
The silence of the sea!

All in a hot and copper sky,
The bloody Sun, at noon,
Right up above the mast did stand,
No bigger than the Moon.

Day after day, day after day,
We stuck, nor breath nor motion;
As idle as a painted ship
Upon a painted ocean.

Water, water, everywhere,
And all the boards did shrink;
Water, water, everywhere,
Nor any drop to drink.

From *The Rime of the Ancient Mariner* by
Samuel Taylor Coleridge

Chapter 4
Extreme weather

Who am I?
I began as a brilliant day
So sunny and breezy and warm.
Water rose into the air
Dark clouds began to form.
Winds spiral around
My swirling eye.
I tear up
The sky.
Storm.

Above Earth's surface, air is constantly moving from place to place. From oceans to land. From land to oceans. From deserts to forests. From ice sheets to wetlands.

The type of weather depends on the temperature of the air. This depends on where the air has been, and where it's going.

When the air is cool, less water evaporates from the land or sea beneath. Fewer clouds form. Skies stay clear, and the weather stays dry. A big mass of cool, dry air is called a high-pressure system.

When air is warm, more water evaporates from the land or sea beneath. Clouds form more easily, including big storm clouds. The weather becomes wet, windy or stormy. A big mass of warm, **moist** air is called a low pressure system.

When weather systems meet, they don't mix easily. Instead, they move over or under one another. One of the air masses might get pushed out of the way or trapped close to the ground.

The invisible lines between different weather systems are called "fronts". We can't see fronts, but we can see the changes in weather they bring as they pass over the place where we live! Some weather systems make headlines because they bring such extreme weather.

Tropical cyclones

Tropical cyclones are also called hurricanes or typhoons. They begin over warm oceans and seas. The warm water warms the air above it, creating a low-pressure system. Fast winds begin to blow in a spiral. They suck in more warm air full of water vapour that has evaporated from the warm sea. Towering storm clouds form.

If tropical cyclones reach land, the fast winds can cause terrible damage. Hurricanes can also cause storm surges, when seawater gets pushed much further over the land than normal. This can cause flooding that is even more dangerous than strong winds.

Monsoons

Monsoon weather is caused when air over the ocean stays much cooler than air over the nearby land. The air over the ocean forms a high-pressure system. It begins to move towards the low-pressure system on land. When the two systems meet, air gets pushed upwards and huge clouds form, bringing torrential rain. Monsoon rains can cause flooding, but they are often celebrated because they also bring the water needed to grow crops.

Sandstorms and dust storms

Very dry areas of the world have extreme
storms too. Sandstorms and dust storms happen
when strong winds, such as the winds caused by
a thunderstorm or a cyclone, lift huge amounts
of sand or dust up into the air. The dust or
sand can travel hundreds or even thousands
of kilometres.

It can be hard to see more than a few metres in a sand or dust storm. Breathing in the dust causes health problems. High in the sky, the dust or sand causes clouds to form. It blocks the Sun's light from reaching the ground, and changes weather patterns. The dust can also cause problems when it returns to the ground in a different place, for example, by blocking roads.

Isn't it weird that ...

Europe doesn't get tropical storms?

Tropical storms only form where the surface of the sea is warmer than 27 degrees Celsius. Parts of Europe do have warm seas in summer, but there isn't enough warm water to feed a tropical storm and keep it going. Tropical cyclones that form over warm parts of the Atlantic Ocean near the Equator are sometimes blown north, towards Europe. However, the sea is colder so the storm usually dies down. Rarely (about twice a year) very strong winds and rain left over from a hurricane make it all the way to Northern Europe. This happened in 2017, when terrible weather caused by Hurricane Ophelia reached Ireland and Scotland.

Weather and climate

Weather changes from day to day, but each place in the world has a typical pattern of weather throughout the year. This is known as its **climate**. The UK's climate is **mild** and moist. We expect more sunny days in summer, and more rainy or snowy days in winter. The Amazon rainforest and the Arctic get rain and sun too, but they have very different climates from the UK.

The climate of a place affects the type of plants and animals that can live there. For example, the UK's climate is too cool for pineapples to grow, but too warm for polar bears! Climate also affects the types of crops that farmers can grow, and the types of homes that people build. Weather patterns have shaped the world. However, climates around the world are changing due to global warming. As sea temperatures in the Northern Atlantic rise, more tropical storms could reach Europe, bringing extreme weather more often.

Chapter 5
Tricks of the light

Dismal, rain-soaked sky seen from a different angle reveals a rainbow.

The Sun is 150 million kilometres from Earth, but it is close enough to power all of Earth's weather. The Sun's energy warms Earth's air and water, making winds blow and causing the water cycle, which brings precipitation. Sunlight also brings dazzling displays in the sky.

Rainbows

On a showery day, when sunlight streams through gaps in the clouds, you might spot a rainbow in the sky. You are seeing sunlight that has been split up into its different colours. Usually, these colours are mixed to make white light. But when sunlight travels through water, the colours can get split up.

Isn't it weird that ...

we can't touch a rainbow?

A rainbow isn't a solid object that you can touch, but a trick of the light. If you walk towards a rainbow, it won't get any closer.

To see a rainbow in the sky, you must stand with your back to the Sun and look towards rain clouds. As white light from the Sun passes in and out of raindrops, it gets split up into different colours.

Try this!

You can make a rainbow using water and sunlight. On a sunny day, fill a glass jar or bowl with water. Hold a small mirror under the water. Move the mirror around until sunlight bounces off the mirror and onto a wall or ceiling.

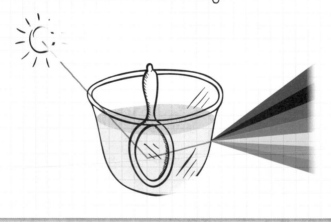

Double rainbows

Sometimes sunlight is reflected twice inside each raindrop, creating a double rainbow. This often happens when the Sun is low in the sky, early in the morning or late in the afternoon. The second rainbow is larger and fainter than the main rainbow. Its colours are also in reverse order.

Some people use the sentence "Richard Of York Gave Battle In Vain" to remember the order of colours in a rainbow (red, orange, yellow, green, blue, indigo and violet). Can you think of a sentence to help people remember the order of colours in a double rainbow (VIBGYOR –Very Interesting Beetles Gobble Yesterday's Orange Rind)?

Moonbows

Moonlight is sunlight that bounces off
the moon before it reaches Earth. This means
moonlight can be split into rainbow colours too.
Moonbows look like a ring around the moon.
They are much weaker and harder to see
than rainbows. Look out for them when there
is a full moon, and thin wispy clouds, high in
the sky.

Sundogs

Clouds can also split sunlight into different colours. When sunlight shines through icy cirrus clouds, you might spot "sundogs" on either side of the Sun. They look like small sections of a rainbow around the Sun.

Light pillars

Lights on the ground can cause strange weather too. On freezing cold days, the air close to the ground can contain billions of tiny ice crystals. When light from homes and streetlights bounces off these ice crystals, it looks a bit like the Bifröst – the famous rainbow bridge from Norse myths.

Polar lights

Sunlight is not the only thing that escapes from the surface of the Sun. Other types of energy and tiny particles also stream towards Earth from the Sun. This is known as the solar wind. When the solar wind reaches Earth, it collides with the thick blanket of air around our planet and causes some strange effects.

As particles from the Sun crash into Earth's atmosphere, the air high above the Poles soaks up the energy and gets excited. As it calms down again, it releases the extra energy as light. This is the cause of the glowing northern lights and southern lights, known as aurora, that are visible in the night sky near Earth's magnetic poles.

Weather places

These places are all named after one type of weather they are most famous for. Which would you like to visit?

Sunshine Glacier, Antarctica

It might seem strange to head to Antarctica to find sunshine, but you won't be disappointed. Even on cloudy days, a patch of blue sky can be seen above the Sunshine Glacier.

Tornado Alley, US

If wind is your thing, visit Tornado Valley in the US. This huge, very flat area of land gets thousands of thunderstorms – and tornadoes – every year. Once, more than 200 tornadoes formed in just one day!

Rainbow Falls, Hawaii
At Hawaii's Rainbow Falls, you can see a rainbow without putting up with the rain! Stand with the sun behind you and gaze at the spray created as the Wailuku River plunges over a lava cave. In the Hawaiian language, the waterfall is called *Waiānuenue*, meaning "rainbow water".

Frostproof, Florida
Florida in the southern US has a warm and sunny climate, perfect for growing oranges. However, weather can always surprise us! In 1894 and 1895, a Great Freeze killed most of the orange trees in the area. Trees growing near Keystone City survived, and the town was renamed Frostproof!

Where in the world?

Tornado Alley, US

Rainbow Falls, Hawaii

Frostproof, Florida

Sunshine Glacier, Antarctica

Chapter 6
Predicting the weather

Bees won't swarm before a storm.

Sea gull, sea gull, sit on the sand;
It's never good weather while
you're on the land.

Red sky at night, shepherd's delight.
Red sky in morning, shepherd's warning.

People have always used clues in nature to help them **predict** changes in the weather. They looked for clues in the sky, or changes in the way that plants and animals behaved. Rhymes and sayings helped people to remember the clues.

Plants don't seem to move much, but watch carefully and you'll see them change with the weather, too. For example, daisy flowers droop and close their petals when rain is on the way. This stops the important parts inside from getting waterlogged.

Try this!

Pine cones also close in rainy weather to protect their seeds. Find a pine cone and keep it on a shady windowsill. The scales will close when there is lots of water in the air, which is a clue that it's likely to rain. In dry weather, the scales open out again.

Isn't it weird that ...
animals can predict the weather?

If you spot a large flock of birds on the move,
a rainstorm could be on the way. Today's scientists
are finding out how this is linked to incredible
animal senses. Birds can hear certain sounds much
better than we can. They can hear storms from
hundreds of kilometres away, which gives them
time to find a safe place to rest.

Why predict the weather?

The weather affects everyone. Snow and ice can make journeys slower or prevent them altogether. Storms can make it difficult to fly a plane or take a fishing boat to sea. Knowing what the weather will be like helps pilots, sailors, fishers and coastguards to do their jobs safely.

We can't change the weather, but we can prepare for it. Accurate weather **forecasts** help with this. If there is going to be a bad storm, people might need to take shelter, or protect buildings from being flooded. If there is going to be snow or ice, councils can scatter salt and grit on roads to stop vehicles from skidding.

Weather forecasts help energy suppliers to work out if wind turbines or solar panels will produce enough power. Weather forecasts help you, too! If you know what the weather is going to be like, you know whether to dress for rainy play or to slather yourself in sun cream.

Who predicts the weather?

Predicting, or "forecasting" the weather is the job of meteorologists. They are scientists who measure how warm, wet and windy the air is in different places. They also measure the direction winds are blowing. Knowing what the weather is like right now also tells them what the weather might be like in the future. Winds that have come from somewhere cold might bring cold weather. Winds from warm places are more likely to bring warmer weather. Winds that have blown over land might bring dry weather, while winds blowing from the sea are more likely to bring rain.

Meteorologists collect information using **instruments**:

- on Earth's surface
- high up in the sky
- in space.

On the surface

Weather stations are collections of instruments on Earth's surface. There are thousands of weather stations around the world, on land and out at sea. They have been built everywhere from the tops of mountains to the middle of Antarctica.

Some weather stations have simple instruments to measure temperature, air speed and how much water is in the air.
Others include radar systems, which beam radio waves into the sky and measure the waves that bounce off raindrops or ice crystals. This can tell scientists the shape, size and speed of storms and other weather.

Up in the sky

Weather happens in a part of Earth's atmosphere that stretches from the ground to almost 15 kilometres above your head! To measure conditions high in the sky, meteorologists fix instruments to aeroplanes and weather balloons.

Weather balloons are giant helium balloons that carry instruments high into the atmosphere. They can float up far higher than a plane can fly, collecting new measurements every few seconds. The data is sent back to meteorologists on the ground.

Eventually, weather balloons POP! The instruments fall back to Earth on a parachute.

In space

Thousands of weather satellites orbit our planet, more than 100 kilometres above the ground. They monitor Earth's weather from high above, using radar, cameras and other tools.

Help from computers

Meteorologists feed all the information they collect into computer programmes, which work out the most likely weather in the next few hours, days, or weeks. The calculations are based on all the information that people have collected about weather in the past.

Meteorologists also compare new measurements to old predictions to see if the computer programmes got it right. If not, they use the information to improve their computer models.

Weather symbols

Meteorologists use maps and symbols to make weather forecasts quick and easy to understand.

clear night	sunny day	partly cloudy (night)
sunny intervals	mist	fog
cloudy	overcast	light rain shower (night)
light rain shower (day)	drizzle	light rain

heavy rain shower (night)	heavy rain shower (day)	heavy rain
sleet shower (night)	sleet shower (day)	sleet
hail shower (night)	hail shower (day)	hail
light snow shower (night)	light snow shower (day)	light snow
heavy snow shower (night)	heavy snow shower (day)	heavy snow
thunder shower (night)	thunder shower (day)	thunder

Glossary

climate the typical pattern of weather in a certain place

estimate roughly work out a calculation

forecasts predictions about future weather

instruments tools for measuring something, or looking at something

mild a climate that does not get very hot in summer or very cold in winter

moist carrying or holding a lot of water

pollen yellow powder made by a flowering plant

precipitation any form of water that falls from the sky, such as rain, snow, hail and sleet

predict make a best guess about the future, based on evidence

weather the conditions you see when you look out of the window

Index

About the author

Isabel Thomas

Why did you want to be an author?
I loved science and maths, but I also enjoyed writing and performing. I wanted to find a job that combined all of my favourite things.

How did you get into writing?
I began at primary school, by making a book about each school trip or holiday I went on. When I was a teenager, I worked on a student newspaper. Then I got a job with a publisher of maths and science textbooks. At the same time, I began to send publishers my own ideas. If they said "no thank you", I did not give up. I sent them a new idea! If you keep doing this then one day they will have to say yes …

What is it like for you to write?
When writing is going well, it feels like putting a jigsaw puzzle together. I try out different things and change things until I feel like I've got a word or a sentence just right. When writing is going badly, it is hard to sit still at my computer. I have to force myself to put some words on the page. When the page is no longer blank, it starts to feel easier.

What book do you remember reading when you were young?
We had a nature encyclopaedia that I loved because it told stories of plants and animals and helped me answer my questions about the world.

Why did you write this book?

You don't have to travel far to find amazing things. We are surrounded by them! Weather is a really good example. When we start to find out where our weather comes from, we realise how connected we are to everywhere else on the planet.

How do you research a non-fiction book?

I ask questions (sensible questions and silly questions) and look for the answers in all kinds of different places: books and articles written by scientists; videos of different kinds of weather; diaries kept by people who live in different places. I interview experts and I also think about my own experiences.

Is there anything in this book that relates to your own experiences?

I have travelled to every continent (except Antarctica) and have experienced most of the weather in this book. I love thunderstorms! Last summer my family and I got caught in a huge thunderstorm in the high desert in Oregon, in the US. A band let us shelter in their set-up area and we filmed forked lightning in slow-motion.

What's the weirdest weather you've ever seen?

Weather always seems startling when it changes very quickly. In San Francisco in the US, thick fog can roll in from the ocean so quickly it can feel like you have gone from summer to winter in half an hour. Another weird experience was being in the Mojave Desert, so hot that you can feel the moisture evaporating from your eyes.

Book chat

Which part of the book did you like best? Why?

Is there a place you'd like to visit that you've seen in this book?

Which part of the book surprised you the most? Why?

Did this book remind you of anything you have experienced in real life?

What's the weirdest weather you have ever encountered?

What do you think would be the worst weather to experience? Why?

If you had to give the book a new title, what would you choose?

What was the most interesting thing you learnt from reading this book?

If you could ask the author one question, what would it be?

Have you ever seen or experienced any of the weather in this book?

Do you like the name of the book? Why/why not?

What's your favourite picture in the book? Why?

Would you recommend this book? Why or why not?

What more about weather would you like to learn?

Have you ever watched a weather forecast?

Have you ever been taken by surprise by the weather?

Would you like to try any of the 'Try this!' sections in the book? Which one and why?

Book challenge:

Choose your favourite weather from the book and write or find a poem about it.

Collins
BIG CAT

Published by Collins
An imprint of HarperCollins*Publishers*

The News Building
1 London Bridge Street
London SE1 9GF
UK

Macken House
39/40 Mayor Street Upper
Dublin 1
D01 C9W8
Ireland

10 9 8 7 6 5 4 3 2 1

ISBN 978-0-00-862481-1

British Library Cataloguing-in-Publication
Data
A catalogue record for this publication is
available from the British Library.

Download the teaching notes and
word cards to accompany this book at:
http://littlewandle.org.uk/signupfluency/

Get the latest Collins Big Cat news at
collins.co.uk/collinsbigcat

Author: Isabel Thomas
Publisher: Lizzie Catford
Product manager: Caroline Green
Series editor: Charlotte Raby
Commissioning editor: Suzannah Ditchburn
Development editor: Catherine Baker
Project manager: Emily Hooton
Content editor: Daniela Mora Chavarría
Copyeditor: Sally Byford
Proofreader: Gaynor Spry
Cover designer: Sarah Finan
Typesetter: 2Hoots Publishing Services Ltd
Production controller: Katharine Willard

Collins would like to thank the teachers and children at
the following schools who took part in the trialling of
Big Cat for Little Wandle Fluency: Burley And Woodhead
Church of England Primary School; Chesterton Primary
School; Lady Margaret Primary School; Little Sutton
Primary School; Parsloes Primary School.

Printed and bound in the UK using 100% Renewable
Electricity at Martins the Printers Ltd

MIX
Paper | Supporting
responsible forestry
FSC
www.fsc.org
FSC™ C007454

Acknowledgements
The publishers gratefully acknowledge the permission
granted to reproduce the copyright material in this
book. Every effort has been made to trace copyright
holders and to obtain their permission for the use of
copyright material. The publishers will gladly receive
any information enabling them to rectify any error or
omission at the first opportunity.

p8 Minden Pictures/Alamy, p9t Nature Picture Library/
Alamy, p11 keith morris/Alamy, p16l John Sirlin/
Alamy, p16br Lukasz Szczepanski/Alamy, p17bl
blickwinkel/Alamy, p17br Nature Picture Library/
Alamy, pp18-19 onebluelight/Getty Images, p26 Nature
Picture Library/Alamy, p27 SolStock/Getty Images, p39
Courtesy of Stephen Hummel, p40 Courtesy of Paul
McLoughlin, p44 Lars Spangenberg/Alamy, pp56-57
Stefano Politi Markovina/Alamy, p60 DPK-Photo/
Alamy, p61 FOXYPEAM/Getty Images, p62 Ken Gillespie
Photography/Alamy, pp66t and 68b Cindy Hopkins/
Alamy, pp67t and 68tc Sorin Colac/Alamy, pp67b and
68bc America/Alamy, p75 ZEN - Zaneta Razaite /Alamy,
p77 Sinology/Getty Images, all other photos Shutterstock.